INTO THE LIGHT

INTO THE LIGHT

A SUDANESE WOMAN'S JOURNEY THROUGH EDUCATION TO EMPOWERMENT

TERESA SAMUEL

Text Sara Walden, on behalf of Story Terrace

Design Grade Design, London

Cover artwork Eugene Rijn

Copyright © Teresa Samuel & Story Terrace

Text is private and confidential

First print October 2015

www.StoryTerrace.com

CONTENTS

My Late Husband Mr Cleto Hassan Rial Abu Shaka

PREFACE

I am Teresa Samuel Ibrahim and I am an educator, a wife and mother, and founder of charities in my homeland of South Sudan.

Why is my book called *Into the Light*?

Because I have sought out the light of education since my parents encouraged me – a child of poverty growing up in rural Sudan – to go to school and instilled in me the core values I hold to this day.

Because the only light that burned in me from my early childhood was to succeed at school to the best of my abilities and go on to higher education.

Because, against all the odds and in the fog of civil war, I never wavered from my goals of developing in a positive way,

Teresa Samuels

working hard to fight poverty in order to have a bright future for myself and my family.

Because the greatest wish of my adult years was to marry, have a large family and instil in them the same values that I cherish – learning, hard work, dedication to others – and in that I succeeded.

Because, as a mature student and full-time mother, I was awarded a scholarship to study agriculture at the University of Khartoum. My diploma was precious to me, not least because the knowledge I acquired led me to my life's work.

And because, a displaced woman from South Sudan, I was the first to set up charities for the education and empowerment of displaced women and children entirely independent of government or religious organisations. To this day, my charities continue to do their work with the vulnerable and needy.

As I have been guided by the light of so many who have helped and influenced me, I hope, in turn, to bring the light of my people's suffering to the eyes of the world.

1. EARLY DAYS, HAPPY DAYS (1942-1953)

FAMILY AND FAITH IN A SUDANESE VILLAGE

My name is Teresa Omelhassan Samuel Ibrahim. I was born on 17 July 1942 in the town of Wau, Sudan. My family and I lived in an area called Hilat Fellata to the west of Wau town centre, north of the Catholic Mission, south of Mugta and near both a small stream and a spring, *Hanafiat Geti Galbo*, which had been made by the British but named for the Arab who had dug it. It translates as "spring to break the heart of Geti Galbo", and it was a good place to raise a family.

Situated on a small slope, Wau is shaded by mahogany and mango trees. My surroundings were very beautiful, especially during the rainy season when the grass was high and green. We lived in the rich grassland of the savannah, just above the equator, where the air was sweet and fragrant with the scent of the wildflowers and trees, and the flowers we grew near our home.

I loved listening, every afternoon, to the local musicians playing their flutes and beating their drums to the rhythm of their songs. I can still recall my earliest memory. I was two years old and still being breast-fed. Suddenly, my mother stopped. And I wept. Perhaps I remember this so clearly because I rarely cried; I was always one of the happiest children at home and in our neighbourhood.

We lived in a house four metres square, with mud walls and a thatched grass roof. Our bedrooms were shared, with one room for the boys, another for girls and a third for our parents. We each owned one wooden bed, with just mats to spread on the beds and some bed sheets. Each bedroom had a drinking water pot. The water came from a nearby stream or well. It was not until 1960 that water came to the community and then only piped to the houses of the local officials.

We had pets – two dogs and two cats – and some free-range chickens, goats and sheep. My father owned a bicycle and had two donkeys. He rode the male donkey to go to work in the fields and then carried food home for us from the fields. I spent most of my free time helping my mother with domestic work and studying. We had a few books. I enjoyed reading – true stories rather than fiction – and serious conversation. I hated wasting time on nonsense.

I did suffer from hunger in those early days when, after tea in the morning, we had nothing else until our evening meal after school. And I had only my underwear and two dresses, one of which was my "Sunday best". The everyday dress, if it was dirty, would be washed every evening and hung up to dry. Every year, before Christmas, my parents bought me a new dress and then the "best" dress became my everyday dress. I didn't have any shoes.

Despite having little to eat and few clothes, I was able to develop, and I never stopped being a happy child. I didn't need wealth or luxurious food. Whatever we had we enjoyed, with love and gratitude to our parents. My father was a lost boy from Chad, our mother the daughter of a local chief – but still they were poor, and I would weep at my father's struggles to make ends meet.

The only thing that mattered to me was to work hard to fight our poverty and make a bright future for myself and my family. And, in that, I had as inspiration my mother and my father. Let me tell you their stories so you will understand.

I don't know exactly when my father Hammad Ibrahim Ahmed was born but I do know this: that he was only a young boy and living in Abéché in Chad when *bazingir* – foot soldiers sent by a rival chief on a raiding party to capture tribes people from the Borgu tribe and Furs from Darfur to sell to Arab slave traders – descended on the *madrasa* where he was being taught. My father's father, a teacher in the *madrasa*, was murdered. The *madrasa* pupils, my father among them, managed to escape their captors and joined others from other attacks taking refuge in the forest.

Some of the escapees, who had been running through the forest for days, suddenly came across a white man who was hunting near the village of Kafia Kenji. That man was Mr Comyn, the then-British District Commissioner of Bahr el Ghazal province and he saved my father's life. Three boys, including my father, were given medical and other checks, and then taken from Kafia Kenji to Wau, the province's capital 400 miles away, and handed over to the town's Catholic Mission. There, they joined Wau's first and only elementary school, established for the education of the sons of chiefs. The boys were converted to Catholicism and baptised. Hammad became Samuel Hammad Ibrahim.

The boys studied for four years at the school and then trained as teachers under an apprenticeship scheme. They were given food and pocket money and a plot of land each in Wau on which to build a home and a farm outside the town, which the family still own. In return, they became teachers at that school. When the British government later established colonial rule in Wau, Samuel and his colleagues were among the first local staff to work for them. This was the benefit and success of those who campaigned for the abolition of slavery in Africa.

Samuel married a local chief's daughter in Wau in 1930 and they went on to have five children: Natalina Samuel (born 1931), Paul Samuel (1935), Ernesto Samuel (1937), myself and, finally, Rodolfo Samuel (1946), all of whom went on to higher education, married and had children. There is a great physical likeness between my ancestors, my parents and us, passed down from generation to generation until the end of time.

My parents' ancestors on both sides had grown up in slavery and we would hear heartbreaking stories about their treatment by their owners. Fortunately, they were very clever and managed to escape. They owned farmland, where they constructed *tukles* with mud walls and thatched grass roofs and they were farmers, arts and crafters, pottery workers and hunters. My parents and grandparents were ordinary, humble people.

My father was highly educated but from a poor background in Chad, a country known as the poorest in Africa, its people known for their intelligence. My mother, Malindi Morgan Awadi, came from Tonj, where they spoke Bongo. She knew some Arabic because her sisters married Greek merchants in the same town and, as a young woman, she would help out at her sisters' homes. My father spoke Arabic and at home we spoke colloquial Arabic mixed with local tribal languages.

My mother was one of the most important people in my life; although she was illiterate, she supported my father's wishes that all his children be educated. She would help prepare me for school each morning and then accompany me. She encouraged me to be polite and to respect my teachers. When I was only four years old my father encouraged me to go to school even though girls in our society were either forbidden or, at the very least, discouraged from doing so. My parents' support for my schooling was a fundamental reason for my happy childhood.

The church was another important influence and religion played a huge part in my life. We went to church every Sunday and sometimes on weekdays, too. We prayed and recited prayers daily. My father was brought up in and educated by the Catholic Mission of Wau and we, his five children, were given our school uniforms by the church and attended the same Mission school.

I was in the hands of the Catholic nuns from the age of 3 and any time I wasn't at home was spent at the Mission. Aged 5, I was taken by the nuns to visit the sick at home or in hospital, to visit prisoners or to console the orphans at school. I was so impressed by the missionaries' work that I decided I wanted to be a nun when I grew up. We also followed the traditions of the Catholic church because my mother's family lived over 60 miles away and her tribe, the Bonga, was a small one. None of us ever travelled far; we had no means of doing so. Because of the family's poverty, the Mission organised everything for us.

Our father was strict; our education his main concern. We were not allowed to roam the streets. We stayed at home and the family helped and supported one another. We were a very close family.

A PASSION FOR EDUCATION

When I was 4, my father took me to join the orphaned children's playgroup at the Wau mission in April 1947; the southern Sudanese school year ran from April to December. I went on to kindergarten and then spent five years at the elementary school in Wau run by the Catholic nuns of the Order of Comboniani Missionaries of Verona.

In those days, the school system was classified according to either the Italian system – so Elementary was from 5-9 although, in reality, any age was accepted – or Primary, under the British. That continued with Intermediate from 9-12 or 13 (as happened later, when I started teacher training), followed by Secondary – except there was no secondary school for girls then. It was only after UNICEF stated that age should be disregarded that the intake became more flexible.

From the beginning, and although I was born into poverty, I was committed to attending school, graduating and training to work either as a doctor or in the health field or studying agriculture, which always interested me. My core value of caring for others expressed itself in the love I had for my classmates and friends who I helped at school and with their homework, especially those children who were younger and weaker than me.

I would help my schoolmates when they had difficulties with a subject and, later, to prepare for assignments and exams. I was the centre of attention because I was seen as very intelligent; although I was one of the youngest girls, I quickly progressed to the highest class and was always top of the class. My classwork and homework were usually perfect. Although some of my classmates loved me, some of them hated me.

The nuns made me a favourite and the other children made me suffer for it; I was bullied for many years. One day, during break, a classmate pushed me out of a tree. I fell onto my left side and fractured my left elbow. The arm healed well but it was left crooked. You can still see it to this day and it led to one of my nicknames, Om Kinesh ("Om" for mother and "kinesh" for the wooden implement with a bump on one end used in cooking on open fires). My other nickname was T, short for Teresa.

At home, I would clean the bedrooms and tidy the beds early in the morning while the older children went to fetch water. My mother would make the tea that was our only morning sustenance until years later, when my sister married and became able to provide the family with sorghum and then we were given porridge for breakfast at about 11am. My older sister would go to buy food every day; there was no such thing as a fridge. Our evening meal would be boiled meat with okra, *mulukhia*, or another vegetable, and sometimes fish.

I would play with the local children my age who were as young and innocent as I was. I didn't have a best friend; I loved all the children in my group. The neighbourhood boys made simple goalposts out of wood that they had found in the forest so they could play football. I liked playing netball and other games.

We helped our parents whenever we were needed. I sometimes babysat my mother's friends' young children. I also helped pick and chop vegetables. I would go with the family to work in the fields but I found it hard because my allergic eczema made me feel poorly and weak. I suffered from itchy skin and nose bleeds. I was treated with anti-histamine tablets and injections and would recover, but the treatment made me feel sleepy. At the local clinic, there were two nuns trained as midwives who assisted with births and there was a leper colony run by the Mission. For any serious illness, we had the local hospital.

There was no television, but my father owned a radio for the news and other programmes. We chatted, sang songs and told jokes. I would embroider and weave. I often sang, both school and church songs.

My perfect day would begin with going to school from 7.00am to 1.00pm. We lived near the Mission school in Wau and I would walk there and back. Home at 1.30pm, my mother would give me a snack and then I would rest until 3.00pm, when I had more classes until 5.00pm. Back home again, I would wait until we ate dinner together and then, from 8.00pm, I would sleep soundly until the following morning.

I enjoyed gardening. And I enjoyed raising chickens and ducks. I cared for those chickens as if they were my own children and I loved it when they laid eggs, which hatched and turned into chicks. I felt proud watching my chicks grow bigger, adding to my flock.

I played all the school sports, netball being my favourite. In football I was referee and captain, my role model Pelé, but I had to make sure the teachers never caught me – girls were not allowed to play. We all took part in acting Bible stories and I had a role in most of them. I liked to organise my classmates to play games and do role-plays, a community leader even then.

My favourite subjects were English language, mathematics, science, general knowledge and history. The ones I least enjoyed were dance and singing, although I did love to sing this song: "When the bells ring merrily, when the days pass happily, when the hearts are free from sin, praise the name of Jesus, praise the name, praise the name, praise the name of Jesus! When the hearts are free from sin, praise the name of Jesus!" I would put myself in the stories I read, as I did with that song.

I loved history because it tells of real lives, like the civilisation of ancient Egypt, the Greek philosophers and the Roman builders. I read so much history that, even now, I can remember the stories of ancient Rome. And, at home, I loved reading simplified storybooks from the works of Charles Dickens and Shakespeare and Bible stories. I enjoyed my early school days; it was when I discovered my potential. Because I knew Arabic, whatever the subject, the teachers would ask me to translate. They loved me for it, my classmates appreciated it and I felt privileged to help.

I had a good friend in class called Eva Rocco. One day, while we were doing a test and our teacher, a nun, was supervising us, a fly landed on her nose. She kept brushing it away and the fly kept coming back. Eva and I couldn't stop laughing. Irritated both by the fly and our laughing at her, the nun got so angry she chased both of us out of the classroom and told us never to return. The following day I stayed at home – and then the nun sent the Matron to bring us back, saying she hadn't meant to chase us away forever. We apologised to her and that was the last time we were ever mischievous.

Now I want to tell the story of the four friends, a traditional South Sudanese story I was told much later in life by a schoolteacher friend. I like it because it speaks to the need for honesty in friendship and because, all through my life, I always felt there were those who tried to take advantage of me.

Once upon a time there were four friends: a wolf and a dog living in a valley and, beyond the valley, a sheep and a goat. One day the wolf asked his friend the dog to go with him to visit their friends. They set out and when they reached where the sheep and goat lived, they were welcomed and received warmly and spoke of many things.

Then they decided they wanted to go and search for wives in other villages. They crossed valley after valley until, finally, they came upon another valley beyond all the other valleys. As they approached a community, they saw smoke rising and, once there, were welcomed by four beautiful girls whose father was sitting on a stool near the fire, their mother in the kitchen.

The four guests told the girls why they were there. Delighted, the girls told their parents and instructions were immediately given to prepare two rooms – one for the wolf and the dog, and the other for the sheep and the goat. Much to their surprise, the friends saw that their beds were made not only of dry wood but also dried meat. Still, tired from their journey, they went to bed straight after supper. At midnight the wolf woke the dog and said, "What do you think will happen if we eat this meat? These people are wasting it!"

The dog thought for a moment: "Let me go and spy on the sheep and the goat to see if they are eating their meat." He came straight back to tell the wolf that they were. "So, what are we waiting for?" They put the fire out and ate the wood but that wasn't enough. The wolf ate all of his bed while the dog ate some and curled up on what remained. When the wolf saw this, he pulled the dog off and ate the rest of his meat. Of course the sheep and the goat, not being meat-eaters, were only chewing the cud.

The next morning the girls came to clean the sheep and goat's room, removing the rest of the firewood and taking the beds outside. The wolf and the dog's room was a different matter. Both were sleeping on the ground, with the dog curled in the ashes and the wolf snoring on his back. The girls told their parents what they had seen and, when the time came for wives to be chosen, they were given only to the sheep and the goat and not to the wolf and dog.

The four friends started their journey home until, at a junction in the road, the wolf and dog set upon the sheep and goat. This went on until the wolf and dog, badly defeated, ran off. As they approached their home, the wolf said, "What will you say when we get home?" The dog replied, "I'll say we beat the sheep and goat almost to death and that they ran away." "Nice," said the wolf.

By now the two had gone their separate ways and had to shout to be heard. Then the wolf asked the same question again. The dog, knowing the wolf was too far away to reach him, changed his story: "I'll say the sheep nearly beat you to death and you ran away. I, on the other hand, nearly killed the goat but he ran off before I could do it."

The wolf, furious, started chasing the dog, who ran to his house and shut himself inside, sealing the door. The wolf knocked and kicked at the door, to no avail. "That's it," he said. "From now on, we are enemies. If I ever see you, I will eat you. And so it shall be for each generation to come." And that is why, to this day, wolves and dogs are enemies.

My patron saint was St. Teresa of the Child Jesus; she is my spiritual model. I read stories about her life and I lived by her example, and by the example of stories such as the one I've just told you. There was a time when I wanted to become a nun until, when I was 14, I discovered that the white nuns were allowed shoes but the black nuns, because they were African, were told they didn't need them. That was enough to make me decide I no longer wanted to be a nun.

2. WINDS OF CHANGE
(1953-1957)

CIVIL WAR AND CHAOS

In April 1953 I left home for the first time to start class 5 at Mboro Central School, a boarding school in Mboro, 15 miles from Wau. Mboro was an "approved" school, meaning it trained teachers only up to Primary 1 and 2, the minimum level. It was the missionaries who took those of us who had finished Elementary there; the church arranged everything, including transport at the beginning and end of each term.

I was eleven years old and I cried and cried. I was bitten by an ant, fell very ill and wanted to go home – but it was not allowed. We could receive messages and food from our parents but could see them only during school holidays. Towards the end of December an inspector of education, an Englishwoman named Mrs Hunt, visited the school on a routine inspection and found me among the big girls at that college, struggling to cope with the difficult role of teacher training.

At the end of that school year we went home for the long holiday, to return the following April to join class 6, and our final year before graduating as an "approved" teacher. But, as my mother helped me prepare, Mrs Hunt sent a message that I was transferring to Maridi First Intermediate School for Girls in Equatoria, the first of its kind in South Sudan and an "academic" rather than "approved" school.

Training in Arabic was arranged for those girls who were to attend Maridi in Wau, our first introduction to formal teaching of the Arabic language. Maridi is around 300 miles southwest of Wau and that first journey took two long days. I was no longer 13 miles but nearly 300 miles away from home and, at first, it was hard to be boarding so far from everyone I knew. But I quickly grew to love being there and being in higher education. I felt proud of the progress I was making.

It was at Maridi that I met one of my idols. The head teacher, who also taught us English language and Geography, was an Englishwoman called the Reverend Elisabeth Mordecai, who now lives in Leamington Spa.

Summer term over, we celebrated finishing our exams very simply, by going for a walk in the village. We picked and ate wild fruit and came home in the afternoon. I was thinking hard about the next stage of my life. I still had my life goals, which were very important to me. But, just at this moment, I wanted a break from studies, from being forced to become a teacher.

The Girls of Catholic Action and Legion of Mary in Front of Wau Cathedral, 1960

AMIDST FIGHTING, FIGHTING TO LEARN

At 7.00am on 19 August 1955 my life – and that of my country – changed forever. In Torit, the Sudan Defence Force Equatorial Corps mutinied against the oppressive senior Arab officers from the north. Their goal was to liberate the minority Christian southern Sudanese from an increasingly harsh rule, but the coup failed and what was to become the First Civil

Me at Wau Church, Aged 13, 1962

Student Life in Wau

War was to last until 1972, only for a short peace to be broken by the Second Civil War. These wars lasted more than 50 years and those in the south were to be more enslaved, oppressed and impoverished than ever before.

Just one day after the mutiny, its chaos reached the town of Maridi and my boarding school. At dawn I had heard loud shooting and bombardments both terrible and terrifying. The school was in chaos, all of us panic-stricken. I was a third year pupil and just 13 years old. Young as I was, I understood that day that the civil war would put an end to my only goal and desire, that of reaching higher education. I felt helpless and I felt hopeless.

An announcement was made during Assembly that all South Sudan's schools were closed until further notice. Those girls who lived near Maridi could leave, but those who lived further away were not to leave the school until the following January, when we were handed over to American missionaries who had a lorry travelling to Wau and who agreed to take us.

Attending secondary school was out of the question; there was no secondary school for girls in Wau, or in South Sudan for that matter – and just one secondary school for boys, in

Myself, in Front of the Fence of My Family Home, 1962

Myself, Practising on My Bicycle, 1962

Myself, in My Uncle's House, Wau, 1962

Rumbek to the east of the country. But I was determined I was not going to miss out on the chance to have an education. And so, two months after my return home, I paid a visit to the Secretary of Education, Father Trucchi, at his office in the Wau Catholic mission and told him I wanted to join his missionary school called the Nazareth Teachers' Training Centre, seven miles from Wau. It took all my powers to persuade him – and some heated words were exchanged – before he finally agreed.

In April I started my training. I was an easygoing student and happy to volunteer to teach some lessons. I wore ordinary cotton dresses, my head covered with a veil. After school my friends and I would visit each other's homes to eat traditional foods and my favourites, guava and mango. Or we would meet up for an evening walk to the riverside or to nearby villages.

But all was not well. I had been placed in class 6, well below my level. I felt I was wasting my time and I thought more than once about leaving. But where else would I go? The standard of teaching was inferior to that at Maridi and so was the food, sometimes riddled with maggots – not that I cared about that. Father Trucchi didn't like my attitude; I challenged him. His response was brutal: "This" he declared "is the school of the poor". He wasn't willing to help me get better teacher training; he didn't want any of us to progress, and that made me feel like a second-class citizen.

I graduated as a teacher in 1957, the year after I had started, frustrated because I knew that a year's training was not enough. Some graduates did receive their certificates, only for Father Trucchi to take them, tear them up and throw them in the latrine. Father Trucchi did show me my certificate, but he never gave it to me or my fellow trainees, and I realised that the qualification was essentially worthless.

3. OUT IN THE WORLD
(1957-1982)

FIRST LOVE, FIRST HEARTBREAK

It was hard to have a romantic life as a teenager. I was either in school or studying and the only opportunities to meet boys were on Sundays when we went to church.

At Nazareth I had decided for the first time that if someone approached me I would agree to go out with them.

I was one of the very few highly educated girls. There were also a few highly educated male graduate students, and many of them either spoke to me on my way to school or spoke to my family, asking to marry me. But there was no pressure from my parents to marry and I decided, after all, that the only thing I loved was education. I was not interested in marrying, having children, staying at home.

And then I changed my mind. In 1957, the Southern Sudan Students Conference was held in Wau to debate how to progress education after the outbreak of war two years earlier. The recommendations made at the conference were

to allow the rulers of the Arab north to remove the power of the missionaries to run the country's education. Had we students known what the outcome would be we might have decided differently, but we were weaker than the Arabs. They controlled everything.

A party was held for the student delegates after the conference ended. And there I was approached by Christopher Bennet Hatch and fell in love for the very first time, though it was not love at first sight. I was 15 years old and growing up. He was studying agriculture at the University of Khartoum. I felt grateful to Christopher and I loved him very much, not least because he was intelligent and a great scholar. Christopher was from Juba and after he returned home we wrote to each other, not knowing if we would ever receive each other's letters – if the missionaries found letters like ours they would tear them up.

In 1958, I got my first job as an elementary school teacher at Santa Teresa Elementary School for Girls in Wau, where I stayed for five years. The pay was very low – my monthly salary was £S3.60 compared to female teachers from north Sudan who were paid £S9.00 – but I couldn't complain because I knew I was not well qualified. Also I knew that even this would provide a good income for the family and allow us to eat better. I was able to buy my first pair of shoes. They were only cheap, but I no longer had to go barefoot.

Myself and My Classmate Mary Zahra, 1962

At school I was helped by the head teacher, an Italian nun. I enjoyed meeting my pupils and enjoyed teaching, though didn't feel qualified to teach in English after the training I had been given. As a student teacher, I continued my education up to "commercial" level – rather than "academic" – at Juba Commercial Secondary School, with the goal of gaining one of the two places awarded each year to their students to study at the University of Khartoum.

I had stayed in touch with Christopher and in the spring of 1958 when he was on his annual holiday, he came to see me at my home 200 miles away from Juba where he lived. I got a message to meet him at the home of his fellow student Andrew Barjuok. He stood up when he saw me, took me in his arms and hugged me with great affection. I felt shy to receive this, Christopher's first expression of love. A week later he went back home for the rest of the holidays and after that, every week, he sent me letters. Then tragedy struck: I stopped receiving them.

When I asked Andrew what he thought was going on, he said, "Maybe Christopher has lost interest in you?" I was taken aback and I was heartbroken. Then Andrew confessed that he loved me, and wanted to have a relationship with me and marry me. I told Andrew that I had to know what happened with Christopher. Christopher sent me a message telling me that Andrew had taken Christopher's letters instead of passing them on to me. In deep shock, I told Andrew to stay away from me. But it was too late; Christopher was disappointed in

With My Nephew Eliya Palil, His Mother and Aunt Eleni Kiriazi, 1970

me, perhaps thinking I had taken his friend away from him. I blamed the long distance between us. I had lost my first true love, but I soon closed the page of that book and moved on.

A MARRIAGE OF TRUE MINDS

Now I was ready to marry and have children. I was introduced to Cleto Hassan Rial, the man who was to become my husband, by my relatives and his relatives' female friends, who were also my friends. Like Christopher, Cleto was studying a long way away, at Xavier University in Cincinnati, Ohio in the USA, as a graduate student in political science.

We exchanged letters and photos. Letters between us were the only way of being in contact and he asked me to marry him. I was worried that the engagement might go wrong, as my relationship with Christopher had done, and as these kinds of long-distance relationships can. But after long discussions, and with the encouragement of the nuns at my school, I agreed.

We met for the first time just before our wedding. I was already attracted to him because he was intelligent – he was the first South Sudanese ever to obtain a Masters degree, in Political Science from Notre Dame University in Indiana in 1950. But also, once I saw him, the attraction came because he was young and handsome. I loved him for his intelligence. I was intelligent too, and it was important to me to marry a man who would father our intelligent children.

The government took over southern Sudan's missionaries schools in 1959 and my salary increased to £S6.00 a month, although the male teachers were still paid more. In 1960 I was transferred to Nazareth Elementary School. The following year I was to attend skills-improvement training for working teachers at Tonj Primary Teachers' Training Centre, 63 miles away from Wau but I stayed at home while our wedding arrangements were made.

Having trained at the Maridi Institute of Education in Khartoum – transferred there because of the war – I graduated in 1963 as a full primary school teacher, qualified to teach up to Class 6. The Ministry of Education employed me that same year. I earned a good reputation for the training I had done, my hard work and my teaching skills. And, with that diploma, I was at last paid the same as the male teachers. I was happy to finally receive the recognition I felt I deserved.

On 13 September 1963, I married Cleto. We knew only love and happiness and we enjoyed our private times together. My husband loved me with all his heart and treated me with respect. And I had nothing but the greatest respect for him. There were no secrets between us; he never hid any secrets from me. We shared a strong belief in, and love for, education. We were both from poor families but we lived according to our means and our standards. I always respected people who were down-to-earth and humble and we, too, lived our lives with humility.

Three weeks after our wedding we flew to Khartoum, in north Sudan, where Cleto helped establish the Institute of Public Administration at the University of Khartoum. He later joined the academic staff there as a lecturer. We lived in a residential area of Khartoum, in a new home built of brick with a brick fence. It was enough for our small family.

My life had changed profoundly. I was from the rich Savannah grasslands of the south and it took me a long time to adapt to the climate and food in Khartoum. I did eventually get used to the semi-desert climate and the food of the north, which comes from produce grown using irrigation

and fertilisers. The vegetables – indeed, all the food – smelled very different to what I was used to. And I missed home and all my relatives in the south. The people of the north are a mixture of Arab and African; I am pure African.

Not long after we were married and settled in a house that Cleto had rented, I realised that he was broke. We were facing real poverty, but I knew my parents would not get involved because I was married now. I was also pregnant with our first child. I used my savings to buy what we needed, even though the man is the breadwinner in our culture. We went through many hardships in those days and there were no luxuries.

We both worked full time for the government, with Cleto at the university and I at the Catholic Women's Training Centre in Sajan, Khartoum where I taught adult education and primary school training. But I had to stop after four months because I couldn't manage both work and housework while pregnant. Instead, I applied to open a canteen at the local school, hired cooks and people who brewed local beer and, once I had paid rent to the school, the rest of the money was ours. And we survived.

MOTHERING AND TEACHING

On 13 December 1964 our first child, a boy named Emmanuel, was born. He was healthy, but because I wasn't eating

Myself, in My Family House in Khartoum

properly – and there was no-one to care for me – I became seriously ill. And then I contracted malaria, suffering in the dry, hot climate. I was close to death before being admitted to hospital, and put first on a drip, then given drugs by injection. Once I recovered, my strength returned, and I acclimatised to the local climate. I felt so happy and proud to be a mother.

The following year I volunteered and taught at the Catholic Elementary School in Sajana, Khartoum, the same year the white missionaries were expelled from South Sudan. The black missionaries were allowed to stay but were stripped of any power. After our first three children were born, my husband told me he had two other children: a daughter, born in 1958 in El Obeid in the west of Sudan and a son, born in 1960 in Indiana. We did not have enough money to help them when they were growing up, and saw them only once they became adults. Had I known before we married, I would have married Cleto anyway. I was innocent and I had no secrets from him.

By the early 1970s I was a full-time mother at home caring for my family. I had my first five children in Khartoum and the other four children in Juba, southern Sudan. I then adopted my niece and cousin, who lived with us and helped me care for my children, and who I sent to school with them.

I had five boys and four girls in all. My oldest child is Emmanuel Lidime Cleto Rial. He died as an adult, following an illness, while living in the United States. My second son is a

My Firstborn Son Emmanuel Rial, 1970

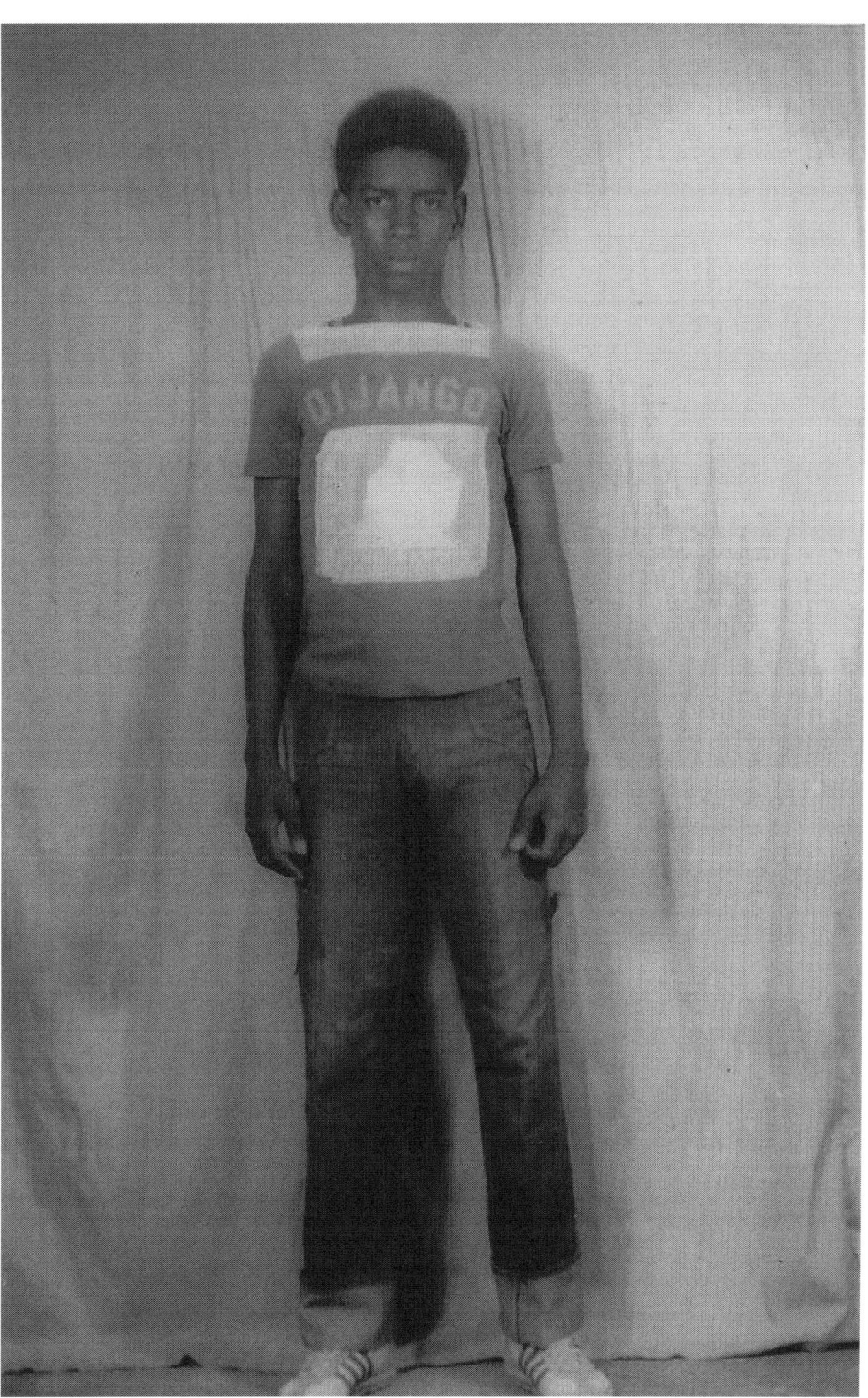

doctor, Isaac Mene Cleto Rial, the third is Sarah Anisa Cleto Rial, the fourth Matilda Zahra Cleto Rial, then Kaidi Cleto Hassan Rial, Aaron Cilagu Cleto Rial, Amos Diffe Cleto Rial, Stella Malindi Cleto Rial and my youngest is Maurice Cleto Rial. I was very happy to have children; it changed me completely. Being a parent is a great responsibility, especially if you have a large family. I was busy with them all the time and left them at home only if there were family events to attend.

My relationship with my husband changed as our family grew. I gave him little attention and he would become frustrated. I would tell him there was no choice, that our

I, Among My Children, 1974   *Myself with My Child*

44

children needed all I could give – and I demanded he help me. I was a good mother, closer to the children and with greater responsibilities than he, but still felt that children need both parents.

At times Cleto and I disagreed about our plans for the future. I wanted to buy a plot of land outside Khartoum to help secure our future, but Cleto was not interested and sat around drinking beer with his friends. So I went ahead on my own. I applied to the government for a plot and had a house built.

In 1972, South Sudan gained regional autonomy. Cleto had been transferred to Juba as first Secretary General of the High Executive Council, the regional government and the following year I moved the family from Wau to Juba. Once settled in my homeland, where the climate suited me, I realised how unhappy I had been living in the desert north, away from all my relatives.

Friends told me that when Cleto moved to Juba he fathered another child, a daughter born in 1970 and the children had also heard it from their classmates. The girl was said to look neglected, her mother unkempt. I have nothing to say or do about this. I just felt bad because Cleto didn't tell me.

Our children attended the best schools in Sudan and continued to grow and thrive. I was proud of my elder children's performance in school activities such as sports and games and their good test results, and would laugh whenever they recounted and acted out stories from their teachers. They would run to me when they came home to show me what they had achieved. I was always encouraging, but I also told them I would need to see an even better result the next time. All my children went on to higher education, including the two female relatives I brought up with my children.

The year after I moved to Juba I registered at Juba Commercial Secondary School to study commercial secondary education as a mature student and I did well. But the demands of my large family meant I had to return to my teaching job at an intermediate school. In 1974 I was promoted to be head teacher in charge of a full primary school, and in 1976 I was promoted to deputy head teacher at a primary school in Bulk/Juba. The following year, in 1977, I became head teacher of a primary school in Hai Jalaba and from 1979 to 1980 I was transferred to Hai Malakal Juba Primary School.

In 1979 Cleto was sent to serve in the Regional Ministry of Administration in Yambio as an Executive Director for Western Equatoria. I was able to transfer to Nabima Yambio Primary School as head teacher until 1982 so I could be with him. In 1983 Cleto was finally dismissed from official duties by the new government of Joseph Lagu, Second Vice-President of the Republic. Cleto was imprisoned on trumped-up charges but was eventually acquitted and returned to Wau. After the years of upheaval caused by Cleto's career, my luck was about to change.

My Children

4. WHEN ONE DOOR OPENS, ANOTHER CLOSES (1982-1990)

A DREAM FULFILLED

A two-year diploma course in Rural Education and Nutrition had been established for government teachers at the University of Khartoum's Faculty of Agriculture and we were told that there was a scholarship available to those who performed particularly well in their interviews and tests. My dream of progressing to higher education to study medicine or the sciences was finally in my sights.

I applied for the scholarship and I felt confident. I passed the test and my interview was so successful the interviewers congratulated me. We were told to come back in three days' time, when a list of those accepted would be posted on the board but I didn't even get to see the list before my colleagues broke the news: I had won a scholarship.

Situated in the centre of the city, the University of Khartoum was founded in 1948, the first university in Sudan and, at that time, the only university in the whole country. State-run, it had an excellent reputation, said to be one of the best universities in the world. The main campus was tall and imposing, a landmark building and a centre for excellence. The students, chosen by merit and regardless of faith, came from all over Sudan, all – including me – very proud to be members of the student body.

I remember that first day as if it were yesterday. My fellow students and I introduced ourselves, were shown our classrooms and took our seats. I was dressed formally in a suit. I chatted with my fellow-teachers from South Sudan and those I had just met from some of Sudan's other provinces; it felt as though we had known each other forever. I was proud to be at this famous seat of learning.

The professors were welcoming, though they seemed unimpressed by some of the southern Sudanese students whose work, I later discovered, had been below standard. However, they were impressed by my first assignment and test. Lectures started the second week and work began in earnest. The professors and lecturers were well qualified and taught us well. I was to become known for being very friendly, warm and outgoing, willing to help any of my fellow-students in sickness or any other time of need. My classmates and professors enjoyed my presentations because, as a qualified teacher, I brought materials along to make the lessons lively and enjoyable. The best was when, acting as my son, the deputy head lecturer and I carried water on our heads. Even the inspectors were impressed.

I was asked to take part in my colleagues' research assignment on the use of the English language in Khartoum's streets and markets, where we spoke to many local people in English and achieved good results. An exchange visit to Cairo in Egypt to visit the Bedouin farmers was organised but, because I was ill with malaria, I was unable to go. I was sorry not to have been able to meet Egyptian people, who are said to be easy to get along with.

I thoroughly enjoyed life in college and studying came easy to me. When I wasn't studying, I socialised with people who were of all ages, very sociable and lived together in harmony. Also, thanks to the work of the missionaries, they were committed, practising Christians.

When I was not on campus, I worked hard to take care of my children and prepare food for us all. I would wake up at 5.00am, prepare breakfast for my children and then wake them up to get dressed for school in time for the 6.00am bus. Then it was my turn to take a bus to get to the university. Our breakfast was a sandwich of egg, *fulmodamas* or some cooked meat. For lunch we ate boiled meat with vegetables and *anjera*. In the afternoon, once the children were home, we all enjoyed the evening meal I cooked, and I would share conversations and funny stories told by my lecturers and the students.

My relatives and neighbours would come for short stays with us, impressed not only by my courage in taking the exams to go to university but by my ability to cope once there as a mother and a mature student.

Although it was a two-year course, I didn't graduate until 1985 due, among other things, to disruptions caused by striking students. The Faculty of Agriculture prepared our graduation and my family were there in the graduation hall when I was awarded a diploma, with credit. I was very sad to leave the university and my fellow-students and we hugged each other with tears in our eyes. But later, at home, we were happy to celebrate with friends and relatives over dinner.

I had graduated from higher education and, unlike my previous experiences, I had such a feeling of achievement to have a proper qualification at last. I had two weeks' rest before I returned to my old job as a teacher; the school had been paying my wages while I was studying. I didn't apply to do a post-graduate course. I had a duty to my school and to my family – and I had had enough of the travel.

Then things took a turn for the worse. The family received the dreadful news that Cleto had lung cancer. After a long struggle, the church agreed to give him enough money for an operation to have the diseased lung removed. He went on to live for several years with one lung.

I was asked to choose between teaching rural education and nutrition in secondary schools or institutes of education or to do the same work in nutrition centres. In 1986 I was made deputy head teacher of Jur-river Intermediate school in Khartoum for internally displaced students and, that same year, I helped the Sisters of Comboniani start training in women's promotion. Both these roles were to stand me in good stead for the next stage of my life.

SUFFER THE LITTLE CHILDREN

Those living in the south of the country had been suffering greatly at the hands of the northern Sudanese and the situation worsened dramatically when southern Sudan moved towards self-rule and thousands were killed, displaced or forced to flee the country. I had grown up as part of a displaced family and knew what that meant. And I knew the only means of empowerment for my people would be education, training and employment.

In 1986, with the Second Civil War raging, many internally displaced people (IDPs) were living in a camp in Mayo on the periphery of Khartoum State. Because of what I had learned about rural education and nutrition and because of my desire to share that knowledge, I invited a group of 36 women from my community to a meeting at my shelter in the camp. I told them I wanted to set up a charity or voluntary organization to help the most vulnerable in the camps. I knew there were international organizations who might support us and volunteers who might help us. We needed funds to begin the process, with each of us making a financial contribution. That first meeting we raised £S50.00, an encouraging start.

We became the founders of WOTAP (Women's Training and Promotion Association), a charity to support and empower women, girls and children, including disadvantaged children, and one that functions to this day. I was the first-ever locally displaced person – and woman – in the history of my country to start a charity by herself without help from the government, the church or Islamic bodies. There were several sites where we could do our work. People had fled to Khartoum. A refugee camp with around 72,000 IDPs was to be set up in Jebel Aulia. After the division of Sudan, we expanded to two centres, the original based in Khartoum and the second in Wau.

First, however, we needed land to build a centre. In 1987 three of us from WOTAP visited the local chief of Dar-es-

Pupils in My School, Jebel Khair Wau, 1998

Older Pupils in the Same School, 1998

Salaam Mayo, near Khartoum. He gave us permission in writing, his surveyors allocated us a piece of land and I paid the chief £S.30 for the plot and permission. We set up shelters of straw, wood and bamboo as temporary structures in the Mayo camp and began teaching literacy to the women and pre-school education to their children.

I was still teaching. That same year, because English language teachers were needed to teach English to displaced southern Sudanese students at intermediate schools in Khartoum State, I began at Nahr el Jur Junior School in Khartoum west. The following year, in July 1988, I was nominated by the Ministry of Education for a nine-month intensive course in teaching English to speakers of other languages (TEFL). Then, from November to February 1989, I attended a three-month course in Natural Family Planning in Rome. I was very proud to be in Rome with five other colleagues from Sudan. We helped each other and enjoyed the cheerful company of colleagues from all over the Catholic world. On my return, I sat my TEFL exams, passed and was awarded a diploma. And a month after my return, Abdelbasit Saabdrat, the Minister for Education, visited the schools for the displaced children and was very impressed by their command of English. He authorised a transfer so I could teach English in secondary schools in Khartoum State and had me promoted to teach English in Khartoum El Gadima High Secondary School for Boys, where I worked for a short period. Later that year the Ministry of Education promoted me from the elementary sector to the intermediate sector, a great personal achievement. But I was still deeply concerned about the plight of the displaced women we had begun to help, profoundly moved by the suffering of my fellow displaced women for whom I had felt great empathy.

The Embassy of the Netherlands invited several local women to a meeting to discuss establishing our own organization or charity. Afterwards, I met Riet Turksma, a staff member at the embassy and a specialist in issues concerning women in development and gender, and applied for funding for WOTAP. The embassy helped me set up my charity within the proper frameworks. They asked me to present them with a written project proposal for funding, with well-defined aims and objectives and gave me £S50.00. I told them I had the catchment area, the women's group and a site to eventually construct a centre, and that we had established a pre-school and already doubled the number of women attending the literacy class from 36 to 72.

The greater picture, though, was grim. Unprecedented high rainfall and flooding, especially along the River Nile in 1988, had caused devastation, the worst hit being the displaced people occupying unplanned areas along the Nile. Families had had to leave behind their property and anything of value. They were living in degrading conditions, the women surviving by scavenging through waste, by begging in the street or, if they were lucky, working as washerwomen and servants.

The numbers kept growing with each new influx of IDPs. Many ended up starving or malnourished because there was not enough food and a critical shortage of cash. And so some of the women started making local liquors and, at first, this offered a real chance to make money. With the government's introduction of Sharia law, however, they were being molested or even tortured for brewing and selling the liquors. Many had miscarriages and some lost their lives in prison. The children left behind went hungry, vulnerable without their mothers' protection. Most of the men had already fled.

Encounter with Pope John Paul II in the Vatican, 1988-89

WOTAP helped Dar-es-Salaam Mayo's women find other ways to make money, starting with small singing groups. Their materials and musical instruments were rudimentary – but that inspired them to start making money for better instruments and to give financial help to those families whose mothers had been imprisoned for making illegal liquor.

From the money we had received from the Dutch, I spent £S30.00 on an 800 square metre plot of land in Dar es Salaam-Jebel Aulia, 15 km outside Khartoum, now a legal settlement. The area of Dar-es-Salaam Mayo, with its population of 72,000, was resettled within three months. The training centre moved to its official site in Jebel Aulia, with the target group continuing to help generate income, and the German charity DED sponsoring both activities and the construction of a new centre.

A FAMILY TRAGEDY, A DREAM DENIED

In 1990 the British Council gave me two scholarships. The first was for a one-term course called Women Mean Business at Durham University, starting in September. This would be my first-ever trip to the United Kingdom and my first time travelling alone.

I flew from Khartoum to Heathrow and I was excited to see London for the first time, though disappointed to have to go directly to Kings Cross station, where British Council staff helped me on to the train to Durham. In Durham, people I had met on the train helped me get a taxi. Still, I was delighted to finally find myself on campus.

But my delight was to be only too brief. A week later tragedy struck the family when I received the worst news of my life: on 5 October, my husband Cleto had died. Two days later, I returned to my home and to my grief. Once again, a dreadful situation served to remind me of the bad luck I had had with my education.

I returned to my charity work. In 1991 my co-founders and I held WOTAP's second meeting at our plot in Dar Es

My First Time in Britain for the course Women Mean Business, Durham University,

October, 1990

Salaam-Jebel. I submitted a larger project proposal to the Embassy of the Netherlands and we were awarded Guilders 47,000 from 1991 to 1994, with the possibility of another three-year grant.

Our literacy classes began in the semi-built shelters in the camp. I organised the training of a number of women as traditional birth attendants or village midwives, and in the fields of health education, first aid and home nursing. We also trained them to raise chickens, cultivate home gardens, in milk and its products, and in general food and nutrition.

Meanwhile, the German charity Bread for the World had also given us $72,000, over a three-year period, to train women in skills such as handicrafts, leatherwork, textile tie, and dye and tailoring. From 1991 to 2006, the World Food Program supported us both with a school feeding programme for the children and with Food to Work for the women trainees. Every embassy in Khartoum offered WOTAP funding and, as part of assistance to NGOs, the United Nations Development Programme, the Food and Agriculture Organisation, and UNICEF helped us.

WOTAP's Wau sub-office was established and, in 1995, began implementing income-generating adult education and pre-education projects in two centres, later expanded and extended to other locations in Wau after many more women joined WOTAP.

5. AND THE GREATEST
OF THESE IS LOVE
(1990-2015)

EMPOWERING WOMEN

In 1997 the British Council in Khartoum launched an initiative to upgrade teachers. I was selected, sat a forty-five-minute English exam, passed and was awarded a full scholarship to one of the Selly Oak Colleges, which was then attached to the University of Birmingham, for a three-month development studies course for those working with NGOs. There were three of us from South Sudan; the other students came from all over the world. The following year, the Department for International Development funded me to attend the International Book Fair in Zimbabwe. I stayed at the famous Monomotapa Hotel in Harare and it was a great pleasure to meet the other attendees.

The year 1998 brought a famine to Sudan that, because of human rights abuses and drought, became a humanitarian disaster. Women were widowed or abandoned by their husbands, and children were either orphaned or unaccompanied and, with no-one to care for them, had no access to food or schooling. Almost all the girls were illiterate; either they did not attend school or left early because of social problems or their parents' inability to pay.

WOTAP joined national and international organisations and UN agencies to help the IDPs, mostly women and children. With the Ministry of Health, we trained 25 IDP traditional birth attendants to work in the camps and, with UNICEF, helped identify and mobilize women eligible for a

Classroom Semi-Shelter Preschool, Nazareth Wau, 2009

rice scheme that would help households in the camps at times when the World Food Program could not distribute.

In 1999 the Embassy of the Netherlands in Sudan awarded me a full scholarship to attend a one-month course at the Royal Tropical Institute of the University of Amsterdam, a training workshop for Trainers in Women, Gender and Development. The same year, DfID funded a ticket for me to attend the Zimbabwe International Book Fair for the second time and Bread for the World funded three staff members. There, I gave a presentation about the stories from our African culture that I had collected and made into a small book, *Fables from an African Background*. The book was exhibited and I was given the title of African woman writer, pleased that Story Teller had become my third nickname; I have always felt that I am a teller of stories.

In Khartoum, the British ambassador's wife Lillian Craig Harris was setting up her charity Together For Sudan, and I was the most outstanding of the 13 volunteers. Then Lillian set up Together for South Sudan, which was seen by the government as a provocation. The security services had been watching me doing WOTAP work for many years, and I had helped Lillian get land for her charity through a local chief. Now both us of began to arouse suspicion.

After Course for NGO Staff, London, 1997

PAYING THE PRICE

I was a regular visitor to the ambassador's residence next door to the embassy, and the gatekeepers would let me in without question. Opposite was the former UK Embassy, no longer in use, which the National Intelligence and Security Service (NISS) used for spying on those visiting. Lillian was now being photographed and threatened by the Sudanese security services, but her position gave her protection.

I had no such protection. In March 2000 I was arrested in the street as I went to the market to buy food. I showed my

ID, was told I had to go with the agents, and was taken to Khartoum 2 police station where I was put in custody for 48 hours and questioned. I was able to let my family know where I was only by sheer chance: one of the security men lived in my neighbourhood and took them a message.

The agents wanted to know if I was giving information to the British about south Sudan. I said that the ambassador's wife was simply a housewife setting up a charity. The same security guard who had helped before was friendly with higher-ups in the provincial government who dealt with political prisoners and they gained my release. I went to the British embassy, where Lillian gave me a visa and Elizabeth Mordecai sent me a letter of invitation to stay with her in the UK.

I had received another donation from BFTW for six teachers, including myself, to attend the 2000 Zimbabwe Book Fair in July, but the pressure on me from the NISS meant I could no longer do my work. I sent the director of WOTAP in Wau to Birmingham University for a term-length course in Development Studies for the staff of NGOs funded by BFTW, and I handed over the charity's work to my deputy.

A NEW LIFE ON TWO CONTINENTS

I left my country in May 2000 and at Heathrow Airport I applied for asylum. Emmanuel was already in the UK as an asylum seeker. I had children living in Egypt who the UN helped to the USA. My daughter Stella was at Heriot Watt University. I got indefinite leave to remain in 2003 and then British citizenship.

My charity work continued. I set up a local NGO, Refugee Women Training and Promotion for England and Wales, with funding from Awards for All and a small amount from friends in the church. Two years later, in 2005, after the signing of the Comprehensive Peace Agreement between the warring parties in my country, I returned to Sudan to find WOTAP no longer functioning; some of the women had even embezzled funds. With the help of the Dutch I started again, with WOTAP

Myself, in the Ruins of My School in Wau, 2009

Another Classroom Ruins, 2011

for women's training and a branch, Mama Teresa's House, running schools in four areas for disadvantaged children, including those with HIV.

In December 2010 I was the proudest I have ever been when my daughter, Sarah Cleto Rial, the Program Director of the charity My Sister's Keeper, won the US State Department 2010 Eleanor Roosevelt Human Rights Award, presented by Secretary of State Hilary Clinton in the White House. My humanitarian values had been passed on to the next generation.

My Second Son Dr Isaac Rial and His Family in Kampala, Uganda, 2015

I always advised my children to follow my example: study to the best of their abilities; work hard wherever they are employed; help their community. Fortunately, they have taken this advice. They have all done well in their studies and achieved either undergraduate or masters' degrees. I also told them to follow the example of what Cleto and I did for them as children for their own children. My advice was and is helpful. Some grandchildren are doing well and some are lazy – but we keep encouraging them.

My Daughter Sarah Cleto Rial and Hilary Clinton at the White House, 2010

I enjoy being a grandparent though my responsibility is a little less than with my children. I always loved having children around me and I love being near my grandchildren, watching them play, laughing and joking together. I often correct the parents on raising the children during my visits; my daughter-in-law doesn't always like what I say. Sometimes they argue but, though they are young, I see the love they have for one another as they look out for and help the younger ones. When I see the older grandchildren help the smaller ones with their homework and then tidy their rooms, it reminds me of

My Last Born Granddaughter Lumaya Morris and Her Mother, 2014

My Granddaughter, Her Mom and Her Grandparents in Their Home in Birmingham

My Seventh-Born Son Aaron, His Partner and Twins Brody and Broyel, Boston, Massachusetts, USA

how I used to be at that age. I see many of mine and Cleto's characteristics in them.

Nowadays I enjoy being quiet at home, reading books. I also enjoy being a registered school volunteer for CAFOD, the official aid agency of the Catholic Church. When I'm back in Sudan I enjoy gardening at our family's home there. I continue to be an entrepreneur, running my own business

My Grandchild

73

Sarah with Her Three Sons, Buojo, Cleto Cuol and Cristopher Cuol,
and Her Nephew Jido, Boston, USA, 2015

Sarah Rial with Her Niece Lumaya Morris, Boston, USA, 2015

My Two Daughters Sarah and Matilda and Their Children, Boston, USA, 2015

Sarah and Matilda with Their Brother Aaron Rial

as an amateur trader. I own a restaurant and I am a landlady. Renting my houses gives me a reasonable income.

MY VISION FOR THE FUTURE

Sarah's award in 2010 brought home to me very clearly how my values and achievements had benefitted my children, the community and myself. I see a good future for my children as they continue to achieve the highest standards of education and success. Because I have put a lot of effort into community and church work, I would like them to take a similar path; indeed, I would like my children to take over my charity and community work when I am no longer here. I am still here, though, to advise them whenever they might need it.

I have deep concerns about South Sudan. We suffered a long civil war. After the 2005 referendum a resolution ended the war and, in 2011, elections took place with the goal of independence from the north. We were overjoyed when this was achieved but the peace has been short-lived. My country is in the midst of a tribal war and, once again, with mass killings, rape, and diseases such as cholera, it is the people who are the victims.

Fifty years from now, I hope that we will be living in a better world, where there are no wars or hatred, no intrigues or double-crossing, with people of all religions living in harmony.

Printed in Poland
by Amazon Fulfillment
Poland Sp. z o.o., Wrocław